I0483443

ANTHOLOGY 'MINDSET'

—— DAVID CHRISTOPHER PLATT ——

RoseDog Books

PITTSBURGH, PENNSYLVANIA 15238

RoseDog Books
585 Alpha Drive, Suite 103
Pittsburgh, PA 15238
Visit our website at *www.rosedogbookstore.com*

ISBN: 978-1-63937-540-0
eISBN: 978-1-63937-582-0

In the Business Marketing world establishing good creditability and terrific marketing skills, and good console with your business associates and unified personnel and marketing of the business world. And of the opening and closing of different jobs different job opening for different people know one job is alike and neither will it be the same job for different people. We have creditability and good criteria to follow on, is important in the business to make sure the information that you are in correspondence between the business major or representative is the right information to keep on top of are game and keep us away from any margin of error.

If you were an employer, how would you select people to work for you? The following activities helps people learn to think like an employer. Imagine that you run a company. Give your company a name and decide whether you make products or provide a service. Then choose the products or services you offer. Next imagine you have been asked to help others in your company to decide which people to hire or not hire. You must prioritize the source of referencing for the employer to Identify his worker and to know that person is the right candidate for the job.

Expectation 1:

First Impressions

First Impressions are important because negative ones are hard to change. One survey of employers found more than 40 percent of the people they interviewed had a poor personal appearance. These job applicants created a negative first impression based on the way they dressed or groomed. It may not be fair, but it is a fact. First Impressions are also based on things such as how well you speak or whether you are friendly.

Expectation 2:

Soft Skills, Expecially, Dependability and Other Personality Traits

Few employers will hire someone they think will be a problem- even if they have excellent credentials. Poor communication skills, unfriendliness, dishonesty, and other personality characteristics are all reasons for being screened out. You probably considered one or more of these things in your reasons for screening someone in or out.

One of the most important things an employer will consider is whether someone will be dependable. Most employers will not hire someone unless they think the person will be dependable. This is often true even if the person has good experience or training for the job. Being dependable means being on time. Having a good attendance and working hard to meet deadlines. It also means you are likely to stay at the job a while. If you convince an employer that you are dependable and hardworking, you may get the job over someone who has better credentials.

Look at your past experience as well as your present situation. If you have been dependable in the past, they know you are likely to be dependable in the future. The information you or your references provide about previous jobs, schooling, and personal accomplishments will be important in helping in helping an employer decide whether you will be dependable. If employers are not convinced, they can depend on you, they probably will not hire you.

Expectation 3:

Job-Related Skills, Experience, and Training

Most employers interview only those people who have at least the minimum requirements for a job. For example, for an office job, they quickly screen out applicants who cannot use word processing software. Related experience and relevant education and training are important to have an order to be screened in and initially considered for the job. (Cite: Getting the Job You Really Want, Sixth Edition A step-by-step Guide to finding a Good Job in Less Time, c 2011 by JIST Publishing Pg.10 - Pgs.13)

Employees look for many questions in candidates. The following list list gives you an idea of the qualities considered most important when hiring a new Employee. Other characteristics may be particularly important to you, your company and the job you are looking to fill this list gives you a good start Identifying them.

(Hardworking:) Hard can often overcome lack of experience or training. You want to hire people who are willing to do whatever it takes to get the job done. Conversely, no amount of skill can make up for lack of initiative or work ethic. Although you will not know for sure until you make your hire, carefully questioning candidates can give you some idea of there work ethic, of course hard work alone is not always the end-all be-all of hiring's. People can generate a lot of work, but if work does not align with your business. Start tips or is not with the true scope of there

7

role. Then it was a waste of effort be careful to note the difference as you access your candidate.

(Good Attitude:)Although what constitutes a 'Good', attitudes differ from each person positive friendly, willing to help perspectives makes life all the offer and that much enjoyable and makes everyone's job a lot easier. When you are immaterial candidates consider what they will be like to work for the next five years or ten years. Skills are important, but attitude is even more important.

(Experienced:) Some candidates may argumentatively think they should be hired immediately based on weight on height of their institution diploma. However, they may lack a critical element that is so important, the hiring process. Experience an interview give you the opportunity to ask pointed questions that require your candidates to demonstrate that they can do the job.

(Self-Starter:)Smart people can often find better and quicker solutions to the problems that comfort them. In the world of business work smart are more important than book smarts.

(Responsible:)You want to hire people who are willing to take on responsibilities of their position's questions about the kinds of projects your candidates have been responsible for an exact role those projects played in their success can help you determine this important quality. Finer points like showing up for the interview and remembering the name of the company they are interviewing for can also be key indicators of your candidates' sense of responsibility.

(Flexible/Resilient:)Employees who are multitask and switch directions if necessary, in a seamless manner are real assets to any organization in today's fast changing world.

(Cultural Fit:)Every business has its own unique cultural set of values, the ability to fit into cultures and values is key to whether candidates can succeed with in a particular business.

(Stable:) You do not want to hire someone today and then you find out he is already looking for the next position tomorrow. No business can afford the expense of hiring and the training of a new employee, only to have a person leave six months later. You can get some indicators of a person's potential stability by asking pointed questions about how long candidate worked with previous employer and why they left. Be especially through and methodical as you probe this particular area.

(Cite: Starting In Business All In One for Dummies 2 Edition, A Wiley Brand 6 Books in One:/ Eric Tyson, MBA, Bob Nelson, PHD. et, al. Pg.388 par.4 – Pg.390)

List the People to Contact in Each Group

Most people never guess they have any potential warm contacts as they do. The proceeding worksheets can help you identify many people you might overlook. You may not know some of these people well or at all, but you have something in common with them. Contacting them takes some courage, but you will find most people are willing to help if you ask them to in a nice way.

You can use each group on the proceeding worksheet to create a list of names for your network. And these people can give you names of others to contact.

**Networking with Your Warm
Contacts May Be the Only Approach You Need:**
Networking allows you to begin with people you know. They, in turn will lead you to others you did not know previously. As each person refers you to others, you are an d more likely to get the names of people who are employers. You will quickly find that some of your referrals will supervise people with skills similar to yours, or they will give names of others that who do.

If you create list for each group on your group on your Group of People You Know list, you could end up with hundreds of names. Each person knows other people will refer you to still others. If you keep at it, you will eventually meet someone who needs a worker with your skills, and the contact might very well lead to a job offer. Networking that begins with your warm contacts maybe the only job search method you need. It is an effective technique for finding unadvertised jobs.

Method 3: Make Direct Contacts with Employers-Your Cold Contacts
Although it is less comfortable to do it can be effective to directly contact potential employers you don't know an have been referred to. Called cold contacting or cold calling, this approach usually involves calling an employer on the phone without referral or dropping in without an appointment. Both methods are covered here, along with tips to adapt these approaches for use online.

Develop Prospect list of potential Employers to Contact
"Getting to know Your objectives," that it's the best to target your job search to a specific geographic area. Even if you are willing to relocate. It will help you to know in advance in what sort of place you would like to live. One of the negatives of posting your information on the Internet job search sites is that you may be contacted by employers from anywhere. Although this can create an opportunity to consider, a similar job is probable available where you would rather be.

So lets assume for the purpose that you know the areas where you in witch you prefer to work. Your task than becomes to create a list of employers you can cold contact in that area In any community, the best free listening of employers who need someone with your skills is an Internet or paper version of the yellow pages.

A variety of free Web-based yellow pages directions is available. I like bing's local service at www.Bing .com/local/ because it allows you to browse by category or subcategory, whereas some others require you to know in advance the category's name This site also provides the related Web address, phone numbers, address, and other information of potential employers. The printed yellow pages book is also helpful, particularly for its category listings, but it does not provide Web site addresses or other information. If you are looking in multiple locations. Web sources allow you to find information for anywhere, which is a Big plus if you want to relocate.

Whatever source you use, the yellow pages resources allow you to quickly create large list of employers you can cold call. You can use these sources to identify 10 to 20 employers in one hour via phone or e-mail. Many people, using the phone and the right techniques, have been able to set up one or more interviews per hour! Cold contacting people by via e-mail typically takes longer but can also be effective if you use it in combination with follow -up phone calls.

You might be surprised at how many types of organizations could be job sourses for you. Yellow pages sources list virtually all small and large private employers in an area. Including government and not-for- profit employers.

Here is a four-step process for using
the yellow pages to find potential employers.
1. Find the Index. The printed yellow pages book has an index in the front that list organizations in general groupings, arranged in alpha-betical order. Some online yellow pages provide this, but others do not. For this reason, I suggest that you use a printed yellow pages book as a convenient listing of organizations by type. If you use a Web source, you can then know what groupings to enter in this search field.
2. Select likely target. Go through printed yellow pages index and ,for each entry, ask yourself this question Could this type of organization use a person with my skills?

    If the answer is yes or maybe, put a check mark by the type of or-ganization.

    Prioritize those targets. For the types of organizations that you checked,go back and put a number by each type based on how inter-esting it sounds to you . Use the following scale:

    1= Sounds very interesting
    2= Not sure if interested
    3= Does not sound interesting at all

4. Contact specific organizations. Once you have identified target groups, you can turn to the section of the yellow pages where those organizations are listed or can look them up online. Use the phone numbers provided to call directly and ask for an interview. If the on-line listing provides a Web site address, try to find an e-mail address for the person most likely to hire you and send that person an e-mail.

I include part of the real page from a yellow page index in this section to show how this process works. The person using it is looking for a job as an electrical engineer. The check marks are for the types of organizations that might need these skills. The numbers refer to the job seeker's interest level.

As you can see, this is good process for identifying opportunities you might otherwise overlook- and this only one page from the index!

Although this process sounds easy, making effective cold contacts takes practice. You will learn much more about how to make effective phone calls and cold contacts.

Drop In or Employers Without an Appointment

If you are creative, there are many opportunities to make direct contacts with employers during your job search. For example on your way home from interviews, look for other places that might need someone with your skills, and stop in and then ask to see the person in charge. In smaller organizations, this will usually be the manager or owner. In larger organizations, ask for the person in charge of the department where you are most likely to work.

Many times, you can speak with the person in charge without an appointment. If so tell the person you are looking for a position and would like to speak briefly about your qualifications. If you are told the company has no openings, say you would like to talk about the possibility of future openings. If the boss seems busy, it is often best to set up a time when you can come back. Get his or her business card or name and set a day and time for your appointment.

Although this approach takes courage, it often works. If you make a good impression, you are likely to be considered for a future job- before it is advertised to the public.

Tip:
Nothing works all the time. Sometimes dropping in with an appointment will get you an interview. At other times, you will have to be more creative to overcome initial rejection. For example, if the if the person you would like to speak to is not in, ask whether someone else can help you. Make friends with that person and ask him or her to tell the boss you will follow up by phone or e-mail. Leave a JIST Card for the boss and your new contact. Then contact the boss later and ask for an interview. Your new contact, if he or she likes you, will probably put in a good word for you. Be creative! Learn to follow up, and do not take an initial "no" as a final answer.

Method 4: Use the Internet to Support Your Job Search
I earlier in this chapter that posting a resume or other information on job posting sites such as Monster .com was unlikely to work well for you. However, I did suggest you co this anyway and then use other job search methods to actively develop job leads.

- Use social networking sites to build and organize your network. You might think that you do not have a very big network. But when you start thinking of all the people you have met throughout school and your career, you will be surprised how many contacts you really have. Online social networking sites such as Facebook and business networking sites such as LinkedIn help you find all those people, get caught up, and start sharing what you're looking for (and helping others as well).

- Use online directories for employer prospects. I've already shown you how you canuse online and print yellow pages resurces to identify employers that can cold contact. You can use online yelleow pages resourses to get Web addresses of employers you learn about through networking. Some organizations' Web sites provide list of staff and their e-mail addresses or direct phone numbers, allowing you discover a specific person to contact and ask for an interview.

- Research potential employers. Check out an employer's Web site, if there is one, to get information on what company does. You can also Google a company to get additional information this can be useful to prepare for an interview.

- Research people with whom you have interviews scheduled. You can use LinkedIn (www. Linkedin.com)to find basic professional details about the person you are going to interview with. You might find that you have contacts in common, or some other fact that it will make it easier to make "small talk" at the beginning of the interview.

- Tune in to employers on twitter. You can use the micro- messaging site, Twitter (www.twitter.com) to find and follow people who work at your target employers. You can get a feel for the company's issues and possibility find out a job opening in their early stages. You might even be able to strike up a twitter relationship with someone who can hire you.

- Interact via e-mail before interview. E-mail is a time -efficient way for employers to get information. So, make your initial contact by phone or by e-mail, and follow up with additional e-mail that includes your resume or other information want them to know.

- Say thank you after the interview. You should always say thank you immediately following an interview. Sending an e-mail to do this is fine, but sending e-mail and a mailed note, with a JIST card enclosed, is better for more information, "getting a positive response in each Several Interview Phases."

- Find directions to interview locations. It is essential that you arrive a bit early for an interview. Use www.mapquest.com or another mapping system to find specific directions to get there.

- Access targeted sites for networking and uncovering job leads. Many Web sites provide a community of people with similar skills or interest to your own. For example, try to find sites of professional organization that are related to the job you want. See whether you have resources allowing you to post message saying that you are looking for work advice. The point here is to be active not passive, in using the Web to develop networking opportunities and to actively develop job leads.

The Internet is an important tool that you can use throughout your job search in a variety of ways. But keeps in mind that it is a communication tool, not a job search method itself. Use it in sensible ways to support your active search for unadvised job opportunities. Do not waste entire days looking for posted jobs or doing things that will not help you in your search.

Tips for Maximizing Your Job Search Online

Following are some other things you should do to use Internet to support your job search most effectively:

- Clean up your blogs and personal information on the Web. Have you written a journal, blog, or other personal things on the Web? If so, make sure you modify them to be acceptable if an employer finds that the Information- or hide them from public views. Also careful about what you post on Facebook. Even if you set your privacy control to let only friends see your whiny status update and risqué photos, those things have a way of leaking out anyway. If you find something unflattering that someone else has posted about you, ask them to take it down.

- Check your e-mail often. You may prefer to use instant messaging more than e-mail, but many employers will contact you by via e-mail. So, check your e-mail daily and respond quickly to any employer messages.

- Use more formal and grammatically correct writing in your e-mail. Text messages and e-mail are often informal but using a casual writing style will not likely create a positive impression with employers. Write your e-mail carefully, and check for correct spelling, grammar, and other details before sending it to an employer.

- Use instant messaging only if the employer interacts you in this way. Do not assume that an employer wants your instant messages, because many will see this inappropriate from someone they do not know well. Instead, rely one-mail unless your via instant messaging.

Method 5: Send Thank-You Notes and Follow Up
Following up is an important part of the job search. Send a thank- you e-mail or note after you talk with an employer or anyone in your network. Mention that you will contact him or her again at a certain date and time to answer any other questions. Stay in touch in a friendly, polite way with everyone on your network list. Following up and thanking people who will help you is good manners. It is also likely to help you in your job search.

More than just courtesy
Writing a thank-you letter after an interview doesn't just showcase a candidate's manners- it can also make or break someone's chances of landing a job. Nearly 15 percent of hiring managers say they would not hire someone who would not send out a thank-you letter after the interview Thirty two percent sayed they would still consider the candidate but would think less of him or her according to careerbuilder.com "How To Get in the Front Door" survey

Get the Most Out of
Less Effective Job Search Methods

The more effective job methods tend to be active rather than passive. For Example, posting your resume online or filling out an application is passive because it requires an employer to contact you back. More active approaches include contacting the employer directly and asking for an interview. You can do this by walking in and asking for the manager, using the phone and asking for an appointment, or sending an e-mail requesting an interview.

Passive job search methods may result in an employer not contacting you at all. Think about it. If you fill out any application and leave, you may never hear from that employer. But if you drop in and ask to talk to the person who does the hiring, you are more likely to get an interview right then.

Whatever job search methods you use. Your objective is to get an interview. This section helps you look for ways to make any method work better in getting you directly to the person who is most likely to hire or supervise someone with your skills.

The Most Frequently Used Passive Methods
Don't allow yourself to be passive in your search for a job. Even with passive job search methods, there are things to do to increase your chances. Here are some of the more frequent of used passive methods, along with tips to increase their effectiveness.

Employment Agencies
Private employment agencies are businesses that charge a fee either to you or to the employer who hires you. You often see their ads in the help wanted section of the newspaper and in the yellow pages. Fees can be from less than one month 's pay to 15 percent or more of your annual salary.

Be careful about using fee-based employment agencies. Research indicates that more people use and benefit from fee-based agencies than in the past. But you need to realize that relatively few people who register with private agencies get job through them.

When should you use an agency and when shouldn't you? The following tips may be helpful in deciding:

If your skills are in demand and you have a clear job objective, an agency's is more likely to help you.

For example, an experienced accountant, medical technician, or carpenter is more likely to get good results than a teacher ready to change careers or a new graduate.

Request employer-paid job leads. Ask the agency for only job leads where the employer pays the fee. Unless the employer pays the fee, for profit employment agency can be expensive and is not a good idea for most people.

Save money doing your own job search. Many agency workers find their clients jobs the same way you can- by calling employers. Agencies get at least some of there postings by calling employers and asking whether they have any job openings. You can do the same thing yourself, so consider doing the work and saving a bundle.

to accept any job they can talk you into so they can collect their fee. If you feel pressured to take any job, say what you want to think about it overnight and then decide whether you want it.

Be weary of want ads placed by agencies. The agencies advertise an enticing position in the newspaper. Then you find out that the advertised position is not available, and the agency may refer you to a less desirable job.

Check out agencies" Web sites. Most private employment agencies have Web sites. Many of the larger ones have Web sites that help you understand what they do list their fee structures, and even offer available openings. Online yellow pages listings may include their Web site address.

Continue looking for a job. If you decide to use private agencies, continue to look for jobs on your own. Legitimate agencies should not require you to pay a fee for a job you find yourself or limit your job search in any way. Look for agencies that specialize in the types of jobs you want. If you decide to use their services, continue actively look for other openings at the same time.

Not all employment agencies are interested in helping the unemployed. Executive search firms and Headhunters are specialized agencies paid by employers to find already- employed people with excellent work histories. With few exceptions, they are not interested in unemployed people who are looking for jobs.

Government "Career One Stop" Centers

Every state is required to process unemployment compensation claims and provide free employment assistance. While services vary from site to site, many of these centers provide a wide range of services.Services can include career resourses, access to computers and copy machine, career interest and skills testing, job search and job readiness workshops. Youth services, help with finding child care and other community service services, GED and English proficiency assistance, training and education funding, help with resume preparation and Web posting computer access to job listings placed anywhere in the country. And all their services are free!

There are about 2,000 comprehensives plus another 15,000 "affiliate" One- stop programs nationwide. Because services can vary enormously by location, it is important to find out what your local center does and then use whatever services you can. You can locate the nearest centers by going to www.careeronestop.org.

After you find the program, plan to check out the services in person at the beginning of your job search. You may also be eligible for programs that help people with disabilities, veterans, laid off workers, youth, older workers, women, the economically disadvantage, and other groups.

Help- Want Ads

Because help- want ads are now on the Web, too ,even more people can find out about them, making the competition for these jobs even greater. Still, some people do get jobs this way, so go ahead and apply for help- wanted ads in the newspapers. Just be sure to spend most of your time using methods that are more effective. Here are some tips to increase your effectiveness using the source of job leads;

Read Help- Want ads on a Regular basis. The Sunday and Wednesday editions have the most ads (although they have shrunk drastically in recent years). Look at every ad, because jobs of interest may not be listed in an obvious way. For example an accounting job could be listed under "Bookkeeper," "accountant," "controller," or some other heading.

Read the ads online. If your newspaper lists its want ads online, it will probably tell you what Web site it uses. You may be able to get new ads there before there they hit the print addition, and you can probably sort the ads for keywords, date posted, and other criteria.

Respond to any ad that sound interesting, even if you do not meet one or more of its requirements. Employers sometime list skills, educational requirements, or other credentials they do not require to screen out candidates. For example, they may say "college degree required" but end up hiring someone with good experience but no degree.

Try to contact the employer directly. Instead of sending a resume like the ad requests, call and ask for the person who supervises the position you want. Then ask for an appointment to discuss the position. The ad may include the company name or Web site, and you can use either to get more information on the organization and perhaps contact the hiring authority directly via e-mail. These more direct approaches sometimes work and can reduce your chances of being screened out.

Look at old ads. Employers that are advertising for one job often have openings for the other they have not yet advertised in the past may still be filled by someone who is not working out, and you could be the only candidate at this point!

Read ads the evening and weekend. Save weekdays for making direct contact with employers.

Interacting with Personnel

and Human Resources Department

There are several things to remember when dealing with human resources (HR) departments:

Only larger organizations have HR departments Few small employers have a separate person or department to handle employee screening. So, if your job search consists of submitting applications and resumes to a Human Resources or personnel department, you will miss out on three out of four job opportunities. Even very large organizations have smaller local operations that do their own hiring without a formal human resources department.

The function of HR departments is to screen people out. You may think that submitting a resume or application following brief interview with someone in the HR department will result in you being considered for current future openings. Not so. You might be referred to a department head if HR has a job posting that matches your skills. More likely, though, your resume will be put into a pile with just a few sent to the department head, who will then make the hiring decision.

At the best, HR departments can set up an interview. Unless you want to work in an HR department, there is little advantage to being interviewed by them. Many employers in larger organizations prefer hiring people who are referred to them that they trust. And many jobs are filled in just this way, before the HR department even knows there is a job opening. If you do get an interview from an HR, the odds are good that the one making the decision will hire someone else who was personally referred or who got passed the HR screening in some other ways. It happens all the time.

If all seems discouraging, think of the positives. While all the other job seekers are going through the HR screening process, you can spend more of your time seeking out smaller employers or using methods that allow you to get past the HR department to the people who actually do the hiring.

Sending Unsolicited Resumes

Most people will not get good results by e-mailing or mailing resumes to people they don't know. Yes, I know that many resume books suggest this approach, but there is little evidence to suggest this method is effective. True, a good resume will help in your job search, but it won't get you many interviews unless you use it in an appropriate ways.

Very few people get a job by sending resumes to people they do not know. It's almost always better to contact the employer in person, through e-mail, or by phone first. Ask for an interview then send a resume.

Make sure you have a presentable resume as soon as you start your job search. Write a simple one at first and use it in your job search without delay. You can always write a better one later.

Give your resume to friend's relatives and anyone else you can think of. Ask others to pass your resume on to anyone they think might know an opening for someone with your skills.

Other Job Search Alternatives to Consider

While most people will use one of the methods. I have already covered here are some other ideas to consider.

Government Civil Service Jobs: Jobs with federal, state and local government agencies are a major part of our labor market. Applying for government jobs requires you to follow specific procedures. It can take a long time to get an interview for these jobs and even longer before you can get an offer. Even so they may be worth looking into.

Find out local state and federal jobs by contacting the personnel divisions for each. State and local government agencies have Internet sites that provide information. You can find federal government job Information at the office of personnel management site (www.opm.gov) and USA jobs at (www.USA-JOBS.com). A book titled guide to Americas federal jobs (JIST Publishing) is another good information source.

Self-Employment: About 12 percent of all workers are self-employed. It's an option you might consider now or in the future. If you want to join the growing number of people who work for themselves, start by learning more about self-employment options. Libraries often many helpful books and resource materials. The small business administration (www.sba.gov) Provides free resources for entrepreneurs. Another good idea is to work in a business like the one you want to start. There is no better way to learn how to run a similar business. If you work in your family business, get education, training, and work experience in a related business to help grow the family business when the time comes take the leadership role.

Volunteering: If you lack experience or are not getting job offers, consider volunteering to work for no pay. Perhaps you could offer your services for a day or a week to show an employer what you can do. Promise that if things do not work out, you will leave with no hard feelings. This approach really does work, and many employers will give you a chance because they like your attitude.

Temporary agencies: Temporary agencies offer jobs lasting from several days to many months. They charge the employer a bit more that your paid and keep the difference, so you pay no direct fee Many private employment agencies now provide temporary jobs as well. Temporary agencies have grown rapidly in recent years for good reason. They provide employers with short term help, and employers often use them to find people they might want to hire later. Temp agencies can help you survive between jobs and get you experience in different work settings, and they may lead to a long-term job offer.

The military: The military is one of the nation's largest employers, 1.4 million people in the various branches, plus an additional 800,000 in Reserve and National Guard units. It also provides free training, education and tuition credits for college courses during and after the service. Almost any kind of civilian job can also be found in the military. Increasingly, technical training can be used for transition to civilian jobs after time spent in the service. You can find additional information on enlisting at www. Today'smilitary.com and on the military's many career and training options at www.military careers.com.

School employment assistance: If you are lucky enough to attend a school that offers help in career planning or job search, find out what is available. If the school offers job listings, follow the counselor's advice and go to any interviews he or she sets up. Never miss an interview that the school sends you to.

Professional association: Many career areas have associations for people who work in that field. These associations are often good sources of information and networking contacts. The Occupational Outlook Handbook (www.bls.gov/oco) lists major professional associations for each job it covers and gives contact information, including web addresses. Consider joining one or more of these groups and use their members as sources of networking for leads.

Apprenticeship: An apprenticeship is a formal program that allow you to learn through on-the-job experience under the supervision of an experienced worker- and get paid. These programs often include formal classrooms training related to the job, from actor, animal trainer, and baker to surveying technician, truck driver, and well and core drill operators there are more than 600 registered apprenticeship, including one or more that may interest you. An excellent resource this is 200 Best jobs Through Apprenticeship (JIST Publishing) or use the Web site at www.doleta.gov/Oa/eta_default.cfm that is run by the federal government.

Be Creative and Well Organized

in Your Job Search

Reading this book will help you better prepared for the job search than most of your competition. This is good news because employers will often be willing to hire those who present themselves well in the job search and interview over others with better credentials.

But how you spend your time in the job search and what techniques you use will be up to you. Those who get jobs in less time tend to use a variety of job search methods, not just one or two. You just never know what will end up working for you, so plan to use a variety of methods and follow up quickly on any leads.

Spending full time on your job search will be difficult If you are going to school or working, but plan to spend as much time as you can. If you are in school or a training program now, start getting interviews before you finish. The best situation is to already have a job lined up soon after you graduate. If you don't have a positioned lined up before then, decide in advance that you will make getting a job a full-time job as soon as you complete your program.

Although I have covered a variety of job search techniques you should look for creative opportunities throughout you job search. So, feel free to adapt what I present in this book to suit your personality. Be willing to try new things that may intimidate you, and do not give up.

As you continue through this book, here are some key points to remember:

- Most jobs are not advertised.
- Use a variety of job seeking methods.
- Some of your best leads will come from people you know.
- You do not have to wait for a job opening before contacting a potential employer.
- Always try direct contact with the person who will hire you.
- Follow up!

Getting and Using Your Resume, Cover Letter, Portfolio and JIST Card:
Even through a resume by itself will not get you a Job you still need to have one these thoughts keep in mind as it shows you how to right good resume and cover letters and how to condense the important details of your resume into a mini resume called a JIST card. Another way to showcase your qualifications for employers to put into a portfolio.

Resumes do not get jobs done you still need one:
Many Resume books and job research, "experts" tell you that a good resume is important they say a well-done resume may will help you get an interview over others whose resume are not as good. Many Web sites encourage you to post your resume for thousands of employers to view. But resumes by themselves do not get job offers; people do.

While it is true that poorly done resume can get you screened out. A resume alone is usually not a good tool for getting an interview. The best way to get an interview is through direct contact with people. As you learn most from people when the contacts and not just subtle and boring their warm and friendly and truthful contacts or by making direct contacts with employer's which are not warm and unsettle ling contacts or disbelieving contacts.

E-mailing or mailing out lots of resumes is not an effective way to get a job. Posting your resume on job- related business sites may not get you much response either- unless your skills are very much in demand. While almost any job search technique work for some people, the odds are not in your favor. Mass distribution of your resume often delays direct contact with potential employers. Your resume is put on a pile or into a database of other resumes from people who are completing for the same job. Even with a good resume, you are far more likely to be screened -out.

Why You Must Have a Resume:
Although a resume may not be the best tool to get you an interview, you need one for several reasons:

- Employers expect you to have one.
- A good resume will help you present what you have to offer from an employer.
- Using the Internet in job search requires one.

Employers use resumes to find out about your credentials and experience. Covering these details in an interview is not the best use of valuable time. A well-written resume forces you to summarize the highlights of your experience. Once you have done this, you are better able to talk about yourself during the interview. If you want to use the internet to help you look for a job, you need a resume in an electronic format to e-mail to employers and post in searchable database.

The Five Most Effective ways to use a Resume:
Even an excellent resume will not get you interviews unless you use it effectively. The following details on how the best use of your resume to get more interviews.

1. Get the interview first. It is almost better to contact employers by phone, by e-mail, or by in person before you send a resume. If possible, get a referral from someone you know. Or make a cold contact directly to the employer. In either case, ask for an interview. If no opening is available, now, ask to come in and discuss the possibility of future openings
2. Then send your resume. Whenever possible, send or E-mail your resume after you schedule an interview so that the employer can read about you before your meeting. You can then spend valuable interview

time discussing your skills rather than details that are best presented in a resume.

3. Follow up with a thank- you note. Immediately after an interview, thank-you note. Even if you use e-mail to communicate with employers, most appreciated a mailed thank-you note. A mailed note also allows you to enclose your JIST card or another copy of your resume. (A Discard is a mini resume.)

4. Send your resume and JIST card to everyone in your growing job search network. This is an excellent way for people in your network to help you fin unadvertised leads. They can forward your resume and JIST card to others who Might be interested in a person with your skills.

5. Send your resume in the traditional way if you can not make direct contact. In some situations, you can not easily make personal contact with an employer, for example, if you post your resume on the Internet, an employer may contact you first. Or if you respond to a want ad that provides only a post office box number, there is no way to reach an Individual. Go ahead and use those methods, but plan to put more active job search methods.

The Working world:
Does your Resume Match your Background?
According to a survey by preemployment Service Directory, as many as 80 percent of companies perform background checks on potential employees. These preemployment checks only reinforce the need to be truthful with prospective employers right from the start. After all, they are bound to find out anyway, and dishonesty will get foy fired.

Seven Tips for Writing a Resume:
There are no firm rules in writing a good resume. Every resume is different. But here are some tips that are important in writing any resume.

Write it yourself. Look at sample resumes to follow, but do not use their content in your resume. If you do, your resume will sound like someone else. Many employers will guess you did not write it- and that will not help you.

Make every word count. Most resumes should be limited to one or two pages. After you have written a first draft, edit it at least two or more times. If a word phrase cose not support your ability to do the job, cut it Shorter is usually better.

Make it error free. Just one error on your resume can create a negative impression that could be enough to get you screened out. Ask someone else to check your resume for grammar and spelling errors. check each word again before you print your final version. You cannot be too careful.

Make it look good. Appearance, as you know makes lasting impressions. For this reason, your resume must look good, with good design format. All part of good-looking resumes in paper and electronic forms.

Stress your accomplishments. A resume is no place to be humble. Emphasize results. Give facts and numbers and support your accomplishments. Instead of saying of saying that you are good with people, say" I supervised and trained five staffers and increased their productivity by 30 percent. "The sample resumes and JIST cards often include numbers. They make a difference.

Create a simple resume first. Donot delay your job search while working on a "better" resume! Many job seekers spend time improving their resume when they should be looking out for a job. A better approach is to quickly do a simple, error- free resume and actively look for a job. You can work on a better version at night and on weekends.

Keep it lively. Keep your resume short and interesting. Use action verbs and brief sentences.

The Three Basic Types of Resumes

There are a variety of resume styles, but two are most common are chronological and skills resume. Each resume style has advantages and disadvantages. The best resume type for you depends on your situation.

The Chronological Resume

Chronological refers to time. A chronological resume begins with your most recent work or other experiences and move back in time. Two sample resumes for the same person follow. Both are use chronological format.

Look at the first resume, a simple one. Notice how the job seeker's experience is organized. While this resume could be improved, it presents the fact would be an acceptable resume for many employers.

This resume works well because David is looking for a job in his behalf in his present career field. He has a good job history plus related training. Note that he has moved up responsibly. He emphasizes the skills and experience that will assist him in continuing to move up. The resume also includes an applicable skills section. Here David list some of the computer strengths, which are not often included in a resume. This resume would work fine for most job search needs- and it could be completed in about an hour.

This same resume is included in the second example. The improved resume features a prominent job objective and section for sales & marketing experience, education, training, and computer skills. Notice the impact that the added numbers create. This resume may will take an extra hour or two to write. The first resume is fine, but most employers will like an additional positive information in the improved resume.

Money Matters
Retirement reality
Part of getting the job you really want to imagine the time when you will not need a job (or a resume) at all. Unfortunately, the prospect of retirement grows more complicated each year longer life expectancies and rising medical costs only increase the need for a healthy retirement savings. Also, the security blanket of Social Security does not cover as much as it once did. Companies that offer retirement packages, matching 401 K plans and stock options should receive more of your attention that those that do not. Through it may seem a long way off, it is never too early to start planning.

The Electronic Resume:
E mailing your resume as an attached file is the best way to keep your careful format and design. But most resume- posting web sites want a resume with no formatting, just words. This allows them to put your resume into a database so that employers can search for key words. A sample electronic resume and tips for writing one are provided later in this chapter. The best approach is to create standard resume and then modify it as needed electronic submissions.

Writing your resume

Whatever type of resume you choose; you can do many things to make it stand out. Use the following tips to write any style of resume. As you look over the sample resumes in the chapter for idea notice how each resume handles these issues.

Your name and address:
It is often best to use your formal name instead of a nickname. In your address, avoid abbreviations, and include your zip code. If you might move, arrange with the post office to forward your mail to your new address, or use a relative's address on your resume.

Phone numbers and e-mail address:
It is important for employers to be able to reach you, even if only to leave a message. Always include one or more phone numbers where you can be reached. (but not a work phone number). Include your area code and make certain you voice- mail message sounds professional. Most employers will try to reach you by e-mail, so include your e-mail address. If you don't have access to e-mail at home, get an address from a provider such as yahoo and use a library computer to check your messages on a regular basis. And make sure your e-mail address sounds professional!

Job Objective/ Summary:
Include your job objective or career summary in all bu the most basic resume. Look at the examples to see how others have handled this. Notice that David

Dillingham's resume didn't narrow his option by using supervisor," which might keep him out of the running for more such as "responsible jobs.

Education and training:
List job- related training and education and education, including Military training. If your education and training are recent or important parts of credentials, put them at the top. However, people with five or more years of work experience usually place education and training information at the end of their resumes.

Previous experience:
List your most recent job first, and then work your way back. Show promotions as separate jobs. Cluster jobs held long ago or not related to your present objective. These could include the part-time job while going to school. If you have little work experience, list of unpaid work, such as helping with the family business, and volunteer jobs. Always emphasize the skills you used in these experiences that will help you in the job you want now. There is no need to mention that this work is unpaid.

Job gaps:
Your list of work experience may have gaps. You may have been going to school, having a child, or working for yourself, or had other reason for not being traditionally employed. Present this time positively. Saying "self-employed" or "or returned to school to improve my business skills" is better than saying "unemployed" or leaving a gap. You can avoid showering that you did not have a job at certain times by listing years or seasons rather than precise months. For example, you did not work from late January to early march, write your years of employment and not the months. No one else will be able to tell that   you had a two-month hiatus between jobs. For example, A.2009-2010 B.2010- 2011.

Job titles:
Many people have more responsibilities than their job titles suggest. Some titles are unusual and will not mean much to most people. In these cases, use of a title that more accurately tells what you did. For example, shift manager

rather than server if you were in charge of things. Of course, make sure that you do not misrepresent your responsibilities.

Accomplishments:

An employer wants to know about the work you did well and other experiences you had. As you would in an interview, describe some of you best accomplishments. Emphasize the number of people you served, units produced, staff trained, sales increased, and other measurable achievements. Include special activities or accomplishments from other life activities, such as your school club roles.

Personal Data:

This information is optional. Who cares how tall you are or what you like to read? Include personal details only if they directly support your job objective.

References:

Do not list references on your resume. If employer wants them, they will ask. Saying "References available on request" at the end of your resume adds nothing and takes up valuable space.

(Cite: Getting the Job You Really Want, Sixth Edition A Step-by-step Guide to Finding a Good Job in Less Time c 2011 by IST Publishing Pg.92-Pgs.116)

Intermittency

Interestingly a characteristic value of b=1.67, or H= 0.33, often shows up in nature. Kolmogorov 91941) predicted that the change in velocity of turbulence fluid would have b= 5/3. Recent studies of turbulence in the atmosphere by Kida (1991) and Schmitt et al. (1992) have shown that the actual exponent of turbulence is very close to the predicted value. Persistent values of H tend to be approximately 0.70; anti persistence values tend to be approximately 0.33. This suggest there might be a relationship between turbulence and market, volatility. Ironically, when most people equate turbulence with the stock market, they are thinking change in prices. Instead, turbulent flow might better model volatility, Witch can also be bought and sold through the options markets.

Turbulence is considered a cascade phenomenon. It is characterized by energy being transferred from large scale to small scale structures. In turbulence a main force is injected into a fluid. This force causes numerous eddies and smaller eddies split of from larger eddies. This self- similar cascading structure was one of the first images of a dynamical fractal. However, it seems unlikely that this is the phenomenon that characterizes volatility, because it is an inverse power law effect. The Markets are more likely power law phenomena where large scales are the sum of small scales (an amplification process). This amplification process underlies the long- memory process. In volatility, this may be the cause:

1. We have seen term structure of volatility, In the stock bond, and currency markets, volatility increased at a faster rate then the square foot

of time. This relationship of one investment horizon to another, amplifying the effects of the smaller horizons may be the dynamical reason of that volatility has a power law scaling characteristics. At any one time, the fractal structure of the markets (that is many investors, who have different investments horizons, trading simultaneously) is a snapshot of the amplification process underlies the long- memory process. In volatility this may be the case:

2. The stock and bond markets do have maximum scale, showing that the memory effects dissipate as the energy in turbulent flow does. However, currencies do not have this property, and the energy amplification, or memory, continues forever. Volatility, which has a similar value of b to turbulent flow, should be modeled as such.

The well-known Logistics Equation is the simplest method for simulcasting the cascade model of turbulence. The Logistics Equation is characterized by a period- doubling

Route from orderly with this behavior. The Equation is often used as an example of how random-looking results (statistically speaking) can be generated from a simple deterministic equation. What is not well-known is that the Logistics Equation generates impersistent results. This makes it an inappropriate model for the capital markets, although it may be good model for volatility.

The Logistic Equation was originally designed to model population dynamics (as do relaxation process) and ballistics. Assume we have population that has a growth (or "birth") rate, r. If we simply apply the growth rate to the population, we will not have a very interesting or realistic model. The population will simply grow without bound, linearly, through time. As we know the population grows without bound, It will eventually reach a size at witch it outstrips its resources. As resourses become scarcer, the population will decline. Therefore, its important to add a "death" rate. With this factor, as population gets bigger death rate increases. The Logistics Equation contain birth and death rate and takes the following basic form.

The Logistic Equation is an interated equation: its output becomes the input the next time around. Therefore, each output is related to all previous outputs, creating an infinite memory process. The equation has wealth of complex behavior, which is tied to growth rate, r.

The Logistics Equation has been extensively discussed in literature devoted a chapter to in any previous book, but my primary concern was making an intuitive link between fractals. Here I would like to discuss the Logistics Equation as an example of anti persistent process that exhibits, under certain parameter values, the important characteristic of intermittency, as market volatility and turbulent flow do. The Logistics Equation is probably not the model of volatility, but it has certain characteristics that we will wish to see in such a model.

The process can swing from stable behavior to intermittent and then behavior by small changes in the value of r, to return to the population dynamics analogy, at small values of r the position often settles down to an equilibrium level; that its population reaches a size where supply an demand balance out. However r=3.00 two solutions (often called or period 2" or a 2 cycle") appear This event is called pitchfork bifurcation, or period doubling. As r increased, four solution appear, then 16, and then 32. Finally at approximately r 3.60, the output appears random it has become (Amore complete description, including instructions for simulating the Logistic Equation in a common spreadsheet, is available in peters (1991a).

We have seen two model's pink noise. The relationship between relaxation processes and the Logistic Equation should be obvious. Both model populations dynamics as an interated process. However, a similar Equation (13.2) and (13.4) are they also quite different In the relaxation model the decay is due to a correlation time and random event. In Logistics Equation, the decay is due to nonlinear transformation of the popular size itself. The Logistic Equation is a much richer model from a dynamics point of view. However, the relaxation model, with the multiple relaxation times, has great appeal as well, particularly in light of the fractal Market Hypothesis and its view that markets are made up of the superimposition of an infinite number of investment horizons.

There is a significant problem with both models as "Real" models of volatility. Neither process generates the peaked, fat tailed frequency distribution that is characteristic of system $0<H<0.50$, as we will see. In addition, we remain unable to explain why Intermittency and relaxation processes should be related to volatility, which is after all, a by-product of market price dynamics. There is plausible link, but before we can take a look at that, we must take a look at the black noise processes.

43

Black Noise: 0.50<H<1.0

The Hurst process, essentially a black noise process, has already been discussed extensively. Link pink noise, black noise process seems to abound in nature. Pink noises occur in relaxation processes, like turbulence. Black noise appears in a long run cyclical records, like river levels, sunspot numbers, tree ring thicknesses and stock market price changes. The hurst process is one possible explanation for the appearance of black noise, but there are additional reasons for persistence to exist in a time series, we will discuss the possibility of noise and we will examinate fractional Brownian motion.

Infinite Variance and Mean

To most individual who are trained in standard Gaussian statistics, the idea of an infinite mean or variance sounds absurd. We can always calculate the variance or mean of a sample. How can it be infinite? Once again, we are applying a special case, Gaussian statistics, to all those cases, In the family of stable distribution, the normal distribution is a special case that exist when a = 2.0. In that case, the population mean, and variance do exist. Infinite variance means there is no "Population variance" that the distribution tends to at the limit. When we take sample variance, we do so under the Gaussian assumption, as an estimate as unknown population variance. Sharp (1963) said that betas (in modern portfolio Theory (MPT) sense) should be calculated from five years' monthly data. Sharpe chose five years because it gives a statistically significant sample variance needed to estimate the population variance. Five years is statistically significant only if underling distribution is Gaussian. If it is not Gaussian and a <2.0, the sample variance tells nothing about the population variance, because there is no population variance. Sample variances would be expected to be unstable and not tend to any value. Even as the sample size increases. If a <1.0, the same goes for the mean, which also does not exist in the limit.

Characteristics of Fractal Distribution

Stable Levy distribution have a number of desirable characteristics that make them particularly consistent with observed Market behavior. However, these same characteristics make the usefulness of stable distributions questions as we shall see.

Self-Similarity

Why do we now call these distributions fractal, in addition to stable, which was Levy's term? The scale parameter, c, is the answer is the characteristic exponent, a, and the skewness parameter, b, remain the same, changing c, simply rescales the distribution, once we adjust for scale, the probabilities stay the same at all scales with equal value of a, and b. thought a, and b are not dependent of scale, although c and e are. This property makes stable distributions self-similar under changes in scale. Once we adjust the scale parameter, c, the probabilities remain the same. The series- and therefore the distributions- are infinitely divisible. This self-similar statistical structure is the reason we refer to stable Levy distributions as fractal distributions. The characteristics exponent a, which can take fractional values between 1 and 2, is fractal dimension of probability space. Like all fractal dimensions, it is scaling property of the process.

Additive properties

We have already seen that fractal distributions are in variant under addition. This means that stable distributions are additive. Two stocks with the same value of a and b can be added together, and the resulting probability distribution we still have the same value of a, and b although c and d may change. The normal distribution also shares this characteristic, so this aspect of MPT remains intact, as long as all the stocks have the same value as a and b. Unfortunately, it can show different stocks have different Hurst exponents and different values of a. Currently, there is no theory on combining distributions with different alphas. The EMH, assuming normality for all distributions, assumed a= 2.0 for all stocks, which we know to be incorrect.

Discontinuities: Price Jumps

The fat tail in fractal distribution is caused by amplification, and this amplification in a time series causes a jump in the process. They are similar to the jumps in sequential variance for the Cauchy and the Dow. Thus, a large change in a fractal process comes from a small number of large changes, rather than large numbers from small changes, as implied in the Gaussian case these changes tend abrupt and discontinuous – another manifestation of the Noah effect. Mandelbrot (1972, 1982) referred to it as the infinite variance syndrome.

These large discontinuous events are the reason we have infinite variance. It is easy to see why they occur in Markets. When the Market stampedes, or pandemics, fear breads more fear, whether the fear is of capital loss or loss of opportunity. This amplifies the bearish/bullish sentiment and causes discontinuities in executed price, as well as in the bid/ asked prices. According to Fractal Market Hypothesis, these periods of instability occur when the market loses its fractal structure: when long term investors are no longer participating, and risk is concentrated in one, usually short investment horizons. Despite the fact that long – term investors are not participating during the unstable period (because they either left the market or became short term investors), the return in that horizon is still impacted. The infinite variance syndrome affects all investment horizons in measured time.

Cite: FRACTAL MARKET ANALYSIS/Applying Chaos Theory to Investment and Economics, Edgar E. Peters pg. 176 par.2 - pgs.209.

Forecasting and Projections
In business management, you often use forecasting to project sales a process that involves estimating future revenues based on past history. Your forecasts enable you to make estimates of other resources, such as overhead expenses and staffing, that you need to support the revenue team.

The term forecasting, as this book use it, is the result of looking back at the historic data to investigate how what happened earlier determined what happened later. In other words, the process of forecasting takes account of both past and current results and uses that information to project what is likely to happen next.

That might sound a bit like reading Tarot cards, but it is not. For example, economist, physical scientist, and computer engineers have employed these models for decades to forecast (with varying degrees of success) everything from sunspots and the size of skipjack tuna catches to the number of duplicated database queries.

Forecasts that are exactly correct are either very lucky or trivial. Real- world systems always have some element randomness, and no forecasting technique can predict something that occurs on an entirely random basis. However, if there are components in historic data that vary in a way you can depend on, you can use forecasting techniques to make reasonably accurate projections, projections that are better than blind guesses. And that increased accuracy is what reduces your business operational risk.

Unfortunately, business often make an offhand effort at revenue forecasts and let it go at that.

Using Excel, you can forecast many other variables, as long as you reasonable baseline to create forecast. For Example

If your business depends on high- bandwidth telecommunications, you might want to forecast the resources required to keep your users connected to remote computing facilities

If you manage a particular product line, you might want to forecast the number of units that you can expect to sell in the next fiscal year. This kind of forecast can help you determine the recourses necessary to support activities such as installations, warehousing, and maintenance.

If you manage customer service, it can be important to forecast the number of new customers you expect. The forecast might lead you to consider changing your staffing levels to meet changing needs.

Make Sure You Have a Useful Baseline

A baseline set numeric observation made over time and maintained in chronological order.

Monthly revenue totals for the past four years
Daily hospital patients census for the past six months
Average annual liquor consumption since 1970
Number of calls to customer service per hour for the past week

In short, a baseline consists of a set quantity measured over time. From the standpoint of forecasting, baselines have four important technical characteristics:

1. A baseline is ordered from the earliest observation to the most recent. This is fairly simple, even obvious requirement to meet , but you must meet it.

2. All the time periods in the baseline are equally long. You should not mix daily observations with, for example, the average of three day's observation. In practice, you can ignore minor skips. February and March have different numbers of days, but two or three difference is usually ignored for baselines that uses monthly totals.

    The very use of monthly totals implies that such minor differences are not a matter of concern.

3. The observations come from the same point within each time period. For example, suppose your monitoring free way traffic, hoping to forecast when you will have to add new lanes. The conditions that you are measuring are very different on Friday at 5:00pm than on Tuesday at 11:00 am For consistency in the meaning of baseline, you should stick to a particular time and day.

4. Missing data is not allowed. Even one missing observation can throw of the fore casting equations. If a small fraction of you time series is missing, try replacing that data by estimating it.

Moving Average Forecast

Moving averages are easy to use, but sometimes they are too simple to provide a useful forecast. Using this approach, the forecaste at any time period is just the average of the most recent observations in the baseline. For example, If you choose three month moving average the forecast for May would be the observation for February, March, and April. If you choose to take a four-month moving average, then the forecast for May would be the average of January, February, March, and April.

This method is easy to compute, and it responds well to recent changes in the time series. Many time series respond more strongly to recent event than events that occurred a long time ago. For example, suppose that you are forecasting the sales volume of a mature product, once that averages nice, stables sales of 1,000 units per month for several years. If your company suddenly and significantly downsize its sales force, the units sold per month would probably decline, at least a few months.

Continuing the example, if you were using the average sales for the past four months as your forecast for the next month, the forecast would probably be overestimated the actual result. But if you used the average of only the past two months, your forecast would respond more quickly to the effect of downsizing the sales force. The two month moving average forecast would lag behind the actual results for only a month or two.

Therefore, the fewer and more recent the observation involved in a moving average the greater the influence each observation has on the value of the moving average and the more quickly the average responds to changes in the levels of baseline.

You don't want to use a shorter moving average only because it's shorter and it reacts more quickly to the baseline. If your base your moving average forecast on just two observations, It can be trivial (and if you use your observation on the average, its trivial). In particular the moving average will not depict an underlying trend in the data any better than the baseline itself does.

Knowing how many observations to include in moving average is equal parts experiences and knowledge of the data series question. You need to balance greater responsiveness of a shorter moving average against the greater volatility of the average.

One highly unusual data point in three- component average can make a forecast look silly. And the fewer the components, the less the moving average responds to signal and the more to noise. There is no good general rule to use here: You have to use your judgment guided by your knowledge of the time series you're working with.

Making Nonlinear Forecast: The Growth Function
The trend function creates forecasts based on a linear relationship between the observation and the time that the observation was made. Suppose that your chart the data as a line chart with the observation' Magnitude on the vertical axis and time on the horizonal axis. If the relationship is a linear one, the line chart is relatively straight, trending up or down, or it may be horizontal. This is your first often best clue that the relationship is linear, and that trend is probably the best regression- forecasting tool.

However, if the line has a clear upward or downward curve to it, then the relationship between observation and time periods may well be nonlinear. There are many kinds of data that change over time in a nonlinear way. Some

Examples of the data include new product sales, population growth payments on debit principal, and per-unit profit margin. In some cases where the relationship is nonlinear. Excel's growth function can give you a better picture of the pattern than can the trend function.

Cells C12: C14 contain numbers of orders that are forecast for the next three days, if the current nonlinear growth pattern continues. It is smart to temper such optimistic forecasts with some sense of reality, though. When this sort of forecast projects orders that exceed the total site hit, it's probably time to back off the forecast.

Forecasting with Excel's Smoothing Functions

Smoothing is a way to get your forecast to respond quickly to events that occur during the baseline period, in a way that is similar to how moving averages behave. Regression approaches such Trend and Growth create forecast by applying the same formula to each baseline point. Therefore, it becomes quite complex to get a quick response to a shift in the level of baseline without back casting to points before the shift occurred. Smoothing is a useful way to deal with this problem. It resembles the moving average approach in some ways but improves on it by building in self- correction mechanism.

Choosing a Smoothing Constant

You should avoid using a damping factor smaller than 0.7 If exponential smoothing appears to work significantly better with larger smoothing constant, it is likely due to a substantial amount of autocorrelation in the time series. If so, you need to deal with it by means of a forecasting technique other than simple exponential smoothing.

Autocorrelation is an important concept in forecasting. It quantifies a dependency between observation that occur at a given time and observation that occur some number of time period earlier. For example, if you pair up each observation with the observation that immediately precedes it, you can calculate the correlation between the two sets of data that results from the pairings. If the correlation is strong- say, 0.5 or greater- then there is a substantial amount of autocorrelation in the time series, the autocorrelation –

the dependable relationship between earlier observations and ones- is at the heart of autoregression forecast. However, a baseline time series with much autocorrelation does not lend itself well to the simple smoothing approach to forecasting.

Two smoothing constants are necessary for seasonal smoothing. One is for th baseline's level, just as simple exponential smoothing. One is for the seasonal component. You can use Solver, as shown in there to help you find the best values for the constants as the changing cells is solver.

Establishing the Final Forecasts
Speaking of final forecast: The horizontal, seasonal model holds that the level of the baseline does not change, and different values for that level are just Random fluctuation. If that is the case, then at the end of the baseline it's not reasonable to assume that it's level will not change ongoing and forward basis. And that implies that you can add to the level the seasonal effects that were estimated most recently.

Notice that the formula freezes the references g$25 in the twenty- fifth row. It does so by means of the dollar sign before row number 25 in the address. You can now drag for- mula down an additional five rows to take advantage of most recent seasonal estimates that you have calculated in the range H21: H25.

Using the Box – Jenkins ARIMA approach:
When Excel's Built- In Functions Will Not Do
Box- Jenkins methods often called Arima (for autoregressive Integrated Moving Average) models have much more broader scope than simple moving average or regression or smoothing forecast. They can often remove most of the drawbacks of the approaches discussed previously. But they are based on and use those approaches.

Box- Jenkins methods, are also more complex- well beyond the scope of this book to cover in detail. This chapter discusses only the preliminary phase of these methods: the identification phase. Completing the identification phase. Completing the identification phase helps you decide whether to make your forecast using a program written specifically for Box-Jenkins or whether you can choose a regression or smoothing approach that excel supports directly.

The publisher's website for this book includes a workbook with VBA code that will assist you in determining whether a Box-Jenkins model is necessary to forecast you time series properly.

Understanding ARIMA Basics

Suppose you have a baseline of observation that you want to use to make a forecast. Excel provides little in the way of guidance on whether you should use regression approach such as trend or growth, or a smoothing approach such as Exponential Smoothing add- in, to create forecasts from your baseline. Many people choose one or the other ad hoc basis because they might be more familiar with one approach than with another, or they might want to save time by forecasting with a chart trendline, or they might just flip a coin.

Ben Jenkins model provides you with a quantitative basis for deciding between regression and smoothing simultaneously to create the best forecast. The process does this by examining the patterns of correlations in the baseline and returning the information to you that suggest whether a regression approach (in ARIMA, auto regressive) or smoothing approach (in ARIMA, moving average), or a combination is optional.

The Box- Jenkins identification phase, discussed is a formal rather than ad hoc meaning of choosing approach to forecasting. The Identification phase uses these aspects of a time series.

An Autoregressive component: Each observation depends on prior observation (not necessarily the immediate prior observation). An example is revenue from leases, in witch the amount of revenue each month can usually be predicted by the amount of revenue from the prior month. This similar to the concept of auto correlation described previously in the "Choosing a Smoothing Constant "section.

A trend component: The series level drifts regularly up or down overtime. An example is unit sales of a new product that is gaining market acceptance. Eventually, the unit sales figures will become constant, and the trend will disappear, but during the early phases, there often clear, sometimes explosive trend.

A moving average component: In the Box-Jenkins context, this means that the series experience random shock over time. The effect of these shocks may linger in the level of the series long after the shock has occurred.

These three components may exist separately or in combination in any-time series. There are autoregressive (AR) models, moving average (MA) models, and autoregressive moving average (ARIMA) models. In some cases, such as those with trend in the raw series, it is necessary to work the differences between one observation and the next. Then, before forecasting, the observation has to be undifferenced or integrated. Then and I become part of the model: ARI models, IMA models, and ARIMA models. Furthermore, there may be seasonality in the series, leading to (for example) a series that has both a regular and a seasonal AR component, as well as a regular and seasonal MA component.

With all these models from which to choose, how do you select the one that best fits your time series and is thus the best one to use for forecasting? ARIMA jargon refers to this as the identification phase. Early in the analysis, charts called correlograms are created. These correlograms help identify what sort of forecasting model you should use.

Charting the Correlograms

A VBA module can be found in the file named ARIMA. Xls on the publisher's website. This module contains a Macro named ARIMA that creates correlograms, for time series, by examining correlograms you can determine whether you should use one of the complete Box- Jenkins computer programs to complete the analysis or whether you can use an Excel regression function, or the exponential Smoothing add- in , or the seasonal smoothing template described earlier. There are many programs available that perform complete Box-Jenkins analysis; the more familiar ones include R, SAS, and SPSS.

To run the ARIMA macro, have worksheet open that contains your baseline in a single column then take these steps.

1. Open ARIMA.xls, and switch back to the worksheet that contains your baseline observations.
2. Click Ribbon Developer Tab. Than click Macros button in the code area.

3. In the Macro name /reference list box, select ARIMA
4. Select Run

The ARIMA code displays a dialog box where you enter the address of your baseline data, whether to compute first differences, and how many lags you want to view for the autocorrelation. These sections describe the choices in the dialog box and how to interpret output.

You should not use Box-Jenkins models with fewer than 50 observations in the time series. It takes at least this many observations to model the data with any accuracy. In practice, you usually want well over 100 observations before starting your forecast process.

In other words, before you decide to employ these methods with any real baseline data, be sure that you have enough data points to make the task worth your time.

Displaying Forecast Data with Power BI
The charts of actual forecast are generally shown online charts. There is typically one line to show the actual observation, and another line to show the forecasts the chart frequently shows the baseline from the first time period through the end of the baseline, and forecast line does not show up until two or more periods into the baseline. The forecast line usually extends at least one time period beyond the end of the baseline. You also normally see the dates that correspond to the periods along the Horizontal, x-axis.

Summary
Forecasting can be tricky, to create a good forecast, you need well measured, and well- defined baseline of data. You should use the suggestion the most appropriate approach (moving average, regression, smoothing, or Box-Jenkins). At times your baseline might not suggest an appropriate method, and you might need to wait for a longer baseline before you can be confident of your forecast.

Even if you feel you have done everything right, conditions have away of changing unexpectedly, making your careful forecast look like a blind guess. Be sure to regard your forecasts with a healthy does of skepticism. The more variables you have to work with, the more ways there are to view the future. Changes in one forecast can tip you off to the possibility that another forecast is about to change.

In the methods described there are accurate ways to help you build your business plan. They can help you answer questions such as whether to antici- pate an increase or a decrease in demand, whether price ranges are rising or falling, and perhaps more important, to what degree.

Because discussion of the underlying theory of these approaches is beyond the scope of this book, you should consider studying a text devoted to topic such as Time Series Analysis, Forecasting, and control by G.E.P. Box and G.M. Jenkins if you make many forecast in the course of your work.

Cite: Fifth Edition Business Analysis with Microsoft Excel, Conrad Carl- berg pg.215-pgs.255

Actually, people with fixed mindset expect ability to show up on its own before any learning takes place. After all, if you have you have it, and if you do not you do not. I see it all the time.

Out of all applicants from all over the world, my department at Columbia admitted six new graduate students a year. They all had amazing test score, nearly perfect grades, and rave recommendations from eminent scholars. Moreover, they had been courted by the top grad schools.

It took one day for some of them to feel like complete imposters. Yesterday they were Hotshots; today they are failures. Here is what happens. They look at the faculty with our long list of publications 'OH my god, I can't do that. "They look at the advanced students who are submitting articles for publications and writing grant proposals. "Oh my god I can't do that." They know how to take tests and get A's, but they do not know how to do this – yet they forget the yet.

Isn't that what school is for, to teach? They are there to learn how to do things, not because they know everything.

I wonder if this is what happened to Janet Cooke and Stephen Glass, they were both young reporters who skyrocketed to the top- on a fabricated articles. Janet Cooke won a Pulitzer prize for her Washington Post articles about an eight-year boy who was a drug addict. The boy did not exist, and later was stripped of her prize. Stephen Glass was the Whiz kid of the new republic, who seemed to have stories and sources reporters only dream of. The sources did not exist, and stories were not true.

Did Janet Cooke and Stephen Glass need to be perfect right away? Did they feel that admitting ignorance would discredit them with their colleagues? Did they feel they should already be like the big-time reporters before the did hard work learning how? 'We were stars- precocious stars," wrote Stephen Glass, 'and that cheat they did. But I understand them as talented young-people- desperate young people-who are succumbed to the pressures of the fixed Mindset.

There was a saying in the 1960s that went: 'Becoming is better than being. "the fixed Mindset does not allow people the luxury of becoming They have too already been. 24par.10- Pg.25

When people with the fixed mindset opt for success overgrowth, what are they really trying to prove? That they are special. Even superior.

When asked them, "when do you feel smart?" so many of them talked about the times they felt like a special person, someone who was different from and better than other people.

Until I discovered the mindset and how they work, I, too, thought of my-self as more talented than others, maybe even more worthy than others because of my endowments. The scariest thoughts witch I rarely entertained was pos-sibility of being ordinary. This kind of thinking led me to need constant val-idation. Every comment, every look was meaningful- it registered on my intelligence scorecard, my attractiveness scorecard, my likability scorecard. If a day went well, I could bask in my high numbers.

One bitter cold winter night, I went to the opera. That night, the opera was everything you hoped for, and everyone stayed until the very end- not just the end of the opera, but through the curtain calls. Then we all poured into the streets, and we all wanted taxis. I remember it clearly. It was after Midnight, it was seven degrees, there was a strong wind, and time went on, I became more and more miserable. There I was part of undifferentiated crowd. What chance did I have? Suddenly, a taxi pulled up right next to me. The handle of the back door lined up perfectly with my hand, and as I entered, the driver an-nounced, "you were different." I lived for thoughts moments. Not only was I special. It could be detected from a distance.

Shirk, cheat, Blame: Not a Recipe for Success

Beyond how traumatic a setback can be in fixed mindset; this mindset gives you no good recipe for overcoming it. If failure means you lack competence or potential- that you are a failure- where do you go from there?

In one study, seventh Graders told us how they would respond to an academic failure- a poor test grade in a new course. Those with the growth mindsets, no big surprise, said they would study harder for the next test. But those with the fixed mindset said they would study less for the next test. If you do not have the ability, why waste your time? And they said they would seriously consider cheating! If you do not have the ability, they thought you just have to look for another way.

What is more instead of trying to learn from and repair their failures, people with fixed mindset may simply try to repair their self-esteem. For example, they may go looking for people who are even worse off than they are.

College student after doing poorly on a test, were given a chance to look at attest of other students. Those in growth mindset looked at the test of people who had done far better than they had. As usual they wanted to correct their deficiency. But students in the fixed mindsets choose to look at test of people who had done really poorly. That was there way of feeling better about themselves.

Jim Collins tells good to great and similar thing in the corporate world. As Proctor & Gamble surged into the paper goods business, Scotts Paper- which was then the leader- Just gave up. Instead of Mobilizing themselves and putting up a fight, they said "Oh, well… at least there are people in the business worse off than we are."

Another way people with the fixed Mindset try to repair their self-esteem after a failure is by assigning blame or making excuses. Let us return to John McEnroe.

It was never his fault. Onetime he lost a match because he had a fever. One time he had backache. One tine he fell victm to expectations, another time to the tabloids. One time he lost to a friend because the friend was in love but he wasn't. One time he ate to close to the match. One time he was too chunky, another time too thin. One time it was to cold, another time to hot. One time untrained another time overtrained.

His most organizing lost, and the one that still keeps him up all night was his loss in 1984 French open. Why did he loose after leading Ivan Lendl two sets to none. According to McEnroe, it was not his fault. An NBC cameraman took off his headset and noise started coming from the side of the court.

Not his fault. So, he didn't train to improve to concentrate or his emotional control.

John Wooden, the legendary basketball coach, says you are not a failure until you start to take the blame. What he means is that you can still be in the process of learning from your mistakes until you deny them.

When Enron, the energy giant, failed- toppled by a culture of arrogance-whose fault was it? Not mine, instead Jeffrey Skilling the CEO and resident genius. It was the worlds' fault. The world did not appreciate what Enron was trying to do. What about the Justice Departments investigation into massive corporate deception? A "witch Hunt."

Jack Welch, the growth-minded CEO, had a completely different reaction to one of general electrics fiascos. In 1986, General Electric brought Kidder, Peabody, a Wall Street investment banking firm. Soon after the deal closed, Kidder Peabody was hit with a big inside trading scandal. A few years later calamity struck again the form of Joseph Jett, a trader who made bunch of fictious trades, to the tune of hundreds of millions, to pump up his bonus. Welch phoned fourteen of his top Ge colleagues to tell them the bad news and to apologize personally. "I blamed myself for the disaster.

Cite: Mindset/ The New Psychology of Success, Carol Dweck, PHD pg.29 par.6 – pgs.37

How to Think About Stocks and The Stock Market:

In my years of watching the stock market gyrate (and try to explain the gyrations on a daily basis),I have noticed a curious phenomenon that tends to be more common among amateur investors but can afflict the pros as well. In their frenzy to make huge profits, or to avoid huge losses, investors sometimes seem to lose sight of the fact that stocks- and the markets in which they are traded- are not standalone products. These investors talk and act like Microsoft was nothing more than a word that represents a set of moves on a computer terminal or in the stock columns of their local newspaper. They hope the Microsoft number goes up and not down. They toss out names of stocks without knowing what the tiny companies that issued the stocks actually do.

They seem to forget to choose or ignore, that the stocks they are chasing so eagerly represent companies that do something. These companies offer products or services, compete with others that do the same thing and either make a profit or loose money doing it. But to the investors who buy and sell the companies stock, it is not a question of how well the stock is doing.

There is a place in the world for that kind of investor. Indeed, that approach to stock market investing reaches its apotheosis in a company with the unwieldy name of BNP/Cooper Neff Advisor a small investment firm in Radnor Pennsylvania. Each week BNP/ Cooper Neff trades 100 million to 150 million shares of stock on the New York Stock Exchange, as much as the Big boards volume. And it does so without knowing anything about the companies behind those stocks. Cooper Neff traders don't know what a company does, they don't know who the chairman is, they don't know if there making money or losing money. In fact, they don't even know the name of the company. Instead, they rely on complex mathematical algorithms that are designed to remove all amotions from the purchase and sale of a stock.

Andrew Sterge the young mathematical wizard who runs the firm argues that it is a waste of time to try to determine what a share of stock in a company is worth. "There's no god who knows the fair value of traded assets, "he says. "The only way you can know anything about value is how the market tries to find an equilibrium. That's all the market is- a Big feedback mechanism trying to find equilibrium." And the only way to beat the market says MR. Sterge, is to use a computer to trade millions of shares of thousands of stocks in search of tiny inefficiencies. If the computer can be right slightly more than half of the time. The huge volumes and narrow margins turn into fat profits.

But I'm assuming you don't have a computer that Big, or the money to do that many trades each week, or mathematical formulas that will let you capture slight price discrepancies. So if you want to own individual stocks, your going to have to figure out some method of determining witch ones to buy, when to buy them, and when to sell them. It seems fairly logical that the only way to do that is to know something about the company behind the stock.

On Wall Street the research function aimed at knowing all about the company behind the stock is called securities analysis," and its practitioners are usually very smart, well educated, and Highly paid. And they still don't get it right that often in part that's because they're up against thousands of other very smart people all trying to do the same thing, and their collective judgement is at work every minute of the trading day. In effect, while there are as competitive as human beings can get and dearly love to outperform all their competitors, in reality they are all tacitly working together to set a price for each stock and for the stock market as a whole.

The Odds Against You:
The Efficient Market Hypothesis

Before you embark on concentrated effort to learn how to pick winning stocks, or at least before you go any further into the process if you have already started, I want to be sure you are going into it with your eyes wide open. That is why I want to acquaint you with the 'efficient market hypothesis" (EMH). If you accept this hypothesis in its strictest form- that the market encapsulates all knowledge about the values of stocks- then you can willingly give up your quest to out smart the market and devote all the time and effort that would have gone into researching individual stocks to something a lot more fun like coaching soccer, playing golf, or catching fish. Granted, not everyone is convinced that the Hypothesis is correct, at least in its strict form. Certainly, Andrew Sterge at BNP/Cooper Neff would seem to be proof that some in efficiencies are there; if they were not, there would be nothing for his computer and mathematical formulas to find, and the firm would go broke. To be sure there are other more lenient forms of the hypothesis that allow for some measure of individual stock- picking success. Finally, there are those who dismiss the hypothesis entirely, contending rigorous analysis and hard work an investor outsmarts the market.

It only with some reluctance that I have come to the conclusion if the market isn't 100 percent efficient. Taking stance leaves me embarrassingly at odds with some very smart investors- great deal of respect. But it also leaves me with lots of time to do other things than chase stock market returns. And I still have an investment portfolio that is providing me with very pleasing results.

At the heart of the efficient market hypothesis is information. The hypothesis assumes that the vast body of investors will quickly absorb all available information about stock and reflex that information in the price of the stock. The information includes what happened to the company and the stock in the past(earning stock performance in a recession,) what is happening currently(an unexpected change in top management that has just been announced), and what may reasonably be assumed will happen in the near future(in the Federal Reserve has embarked on a course on cutting interest rates, for example that information will be reflected in stock price). No one person has all this information. Instead, each of a thousand investors has bits and pieces and acts accordingly. The sum of their actions is the sum of all knowledge they have- the price of the stock. And the total impact of all that information needs not to be reflected instantly in a stock price. The price can adjust over a period of minute, hours, even days, as the Data are absorbed and evaluated. But do not count on the lag to give you an upper hand. According to the hypothesis, during the time that information is being absorbed the stock price may fluctuate too high or too low- you do not know which- until it settles at a value reflective of all knowledge. Your chances of profiting or loosing on the lag are fifty (simply a random guess). The upshot of efficient market hypothesis in its strictest form is that know single investor can obtain abnormally large profits by knowing by knowing something that other investors do not know.

Obviously, the market is not perfectly efficient. The mania that surrounded the so-called dot- com stocks seem ample evidence of that. But how efficient is it? Adherents of the efficient market hypothesis have devised different ways to describe how efficient the market is that reflect the varying levels of confidence in this hypothesis. At the low end of confidence is the "weak form" of the hypothesis. This maintains only that all past price and volume information of a stock is reflected in the current price of the stock. Thus, knowledge of the past performance of the stock will not be at any use to an investor trying to gain an upper hand since that performance is already reflected in price. This form of the EMH effectively knocks down the entire discipline known as technical analysis which utilizes charts and graphs of the past performance of a stock to predict its future performance.

The next step up acknowledges the effectiveness of the EMH is the "semi strong form." This includes the weak form which assumes that all previous price action is reflected in stock and adds to its assumption that all other current knowledge about a stock in the price as well. This means anything a company does can be known by public, from declaring a dividend to having a product recalled or firing an executive, is quickly reflected in the stock price.

In the United States, where dissemination of information is especially swift and comprehensive, it seems likely that the market is certainly efficient in a semi- strong sense. You might note that this form of the EMH seems to leave room for corporate insiders or researchers to know and utilize for a profit certain aspect of a company that are not known to the public at large. Obviously, insiders might know about developments in the company that are not yet public, but trading on the information is illegal and can costs them both heavy fines and time in jail. And certainly, there are opportunities to dig deeply into the company to find information others do not have. But the EMH does not even let you get away with that. It simply argues that the additional profits such research and permits are, at best, large enough only to reimburse you for the cost of all that research.

The strictest sense of the EMH, the one with which we opened this discussion, is called the "strong form. "It holds for all information, both public and private, is contained in a stock's price. While there are obviously money managers who outperform such well known stock markets measures as the Dow Jones Industrial Average and the S&P 500, the strict form of the EMH argues that they are simply statistical anomalies, their performance being similar to that of a coin flipper who turns heads up ten times in a row. It looks like something besides chance is at work, but in reality, the next flip has fifty-fifty chance of being tails. Likewise, the EMH contends that a seemingly great money manager, even after outperforming the market for ten years in a row, could on any given day begin underperforming the market. In other words, the ability to outperform the market can not be predicted or advanced or sustained forever. Advocates of the EMH concede that there will surely be four or five mutual fund managers who will have produced stunning performances five years from now, far outpacing the market, but nobody can say today who they will be.

Regardless of your view on the EMH, here is a sobering thought to keep in mind: If your smart enough to find in efficiency- a stock that is priced at a low for some reason- and act on that information, you have already helped make the market more efficient. The point is, if there are inefficiencies, somebody is going to find out about them. It may be Mr. Sterge's computers, or it may be hundreds of thousands of individual investors who use the incredible resource available on the Internet to do their own stock research. In any event, if they do find an inefficiency, they immediately take advantage of it, effectively eliminating it. And that the results are inevitable conclusion that if markets are not totally efficient, they are certainly moving that direction.

Which efficient market hypothesis firmly in mind, let's look at the ways in which professional investments managers or brokers will try to sell you on their methods for beating the market. And their sales pitches can be persuasive. There methods sound logical, and certainly bolster that impression by recounting performance figures that show them soundly beating the overall market.

Finding Values in Stock

We'll start with a look at value investing, because, if markets are efficient, value investing doesn't work; only works if they are not efficient. If you continue to develop deeper into stock investments, you may hear some discussing Graham and Dodd. They're referring to the father of value investing, Benjamin Graham, and his chief disciple, David Dodd, who in 1934 coauthored the bible of the value investor, a weighty tome called security Analysis. The Book is available today in the fifth incarnation and contains a wealth of information about how to analyze and invest in stocks and bonds. At $ it isn't cheap, $59.95 and applying its lessons isn't easy. But short of taking university-level course in financial analysis at considerably more expense, it's the single best resource for a determined value investor.

At the heart of Graham and Dodd approach to stock investing is determination of the company's intrinsic value: what the company's worth when its assets, earning, dividends, outlook and management are all considered. Determining the value of each of those factors and adding them up to arrive at a price for a share of the company's stock is not nearly as easy as it may sound. Certain assumptions have to be made about the investment environment, management's, capabilities and value of assets. And once the intrinsic value is determined, it changes albeit slowly, because companies are doing business in a competitive and everchanging environment. Nevertheless, it still remains the goal of the best securities analysts to determine the intrinsic value of the company.

Once the intrinsic value is determined, it is then compared to the company's stock price and judgment is made. If the investor doesn't own the stock, the decision is whether to avoid it or to buy the stock. If the intrinsic is far above the stock price, the decision would to be buy the stock and wait for the other investors to discover up closer to the intrinsic value. If the investor owns the stock, then the decision is whether to hold it or sell it. If the stock price is still below intrinsic value, you would hold, If you stock price is close to the above the intrinsic value you would sell before other investors discover what you have and bid the stock price down to the intrinsic value. The interesting thing about adherents to the Graham and Dodd approach is that they want-indeed, must have- a reasonably efficient market or there is no point to there exercise of determining intrinsic value. But they cannot have a 100 percent efficient market, because that would mean that a company's intrinsic value and stock prices would always be the same, leaving no room to make profits based on all analysis. Instead, value investors argue that stock prices, responding to a variety of factors (not the least of which is the investor' volatile emotions), move both up and above and below intrinsic value, considering with it only occasionally, but usually trending toward it. In other words, they assume if a stock price is higher than the intrinsic value, the stock price will eventually fall closer to that value, it will eventually move higher, to make money, an investor buys a stock when the stock is below the intrinsic value. One can also make money, although at substantially more risk, by borrowing shares of a stock whose price is above the intrinsic value and promptly selling those shares, then buying them back and returning them to their original owner when the stock price falls below intrinsic value, a process called "short selling."

Sounds pretty simple, doesn't it? All you have to do to get rich is start calculating the intrinsic values of bunches of companies then buy stock of companies who is share prices are below their intrinsic value. But, of course, you know if it were that easy everybody would be doing it. And if everybody, did it, they would have already bought up all the stocks trading at less than the intrinsic value less than the company that issued the stock. The market would have become 100 percent efficient, or very close to it. As I said using the Graham and Dodd method to calculate the intrinsic value is itself a complicated process and is possible to get the wrong answer. If you are working with the wrong answer and the other investor has the right answer, you're going to lose money. But there is another problem and relates to the point I made a moment ago, about everybody else doing the same thing: To calculate an accurate intrinsic value for a company, the company has had to been around long enough to have complied a reasonably long series of earnings and price movements. Many such companies have grown so large they attracted lots of attention from Wall Street. In a short, the kinds of companies that are most susceptible to this kind of analysis are ready being analyzed to a fare-thee-well. Do you think those highly paid men and women on Wall Street are going to let you discover something they missed? If they do, they will not be highly paid analyst on Wall Street for very long.

This isn't to say the values of stocks are hard to find at least if Graham and Dodd are correct in assuming that the stock prices react to things like investors emotion. There are times, for example, in which investors in larg numbers become fearful of owning stocks and seem to sell somewhat irrationally. The stock market crash of 1987, in hindsight, was one such period. An alert investor- and one with the courage of his or her convictions- knows stocks in the immediate aftermath of that stunning fall. But it is not easy to be courageous in such circumstances. We recognize long after the event that the 1987 crash was a temporary disruption. At the time some very smart people- including Alan Greenspan, who had only recently to be appointed to head of the Federal Reserve- thought it signaled the beginning of tremendous stress on the Us. Economy. Conversely, more than a few investors regarded the Great Crash back of 1929 as a temporary setback. They suffered the consequences of that misjudgment for more than a decade

If someone can predict accurately what the economy is going to do (I do not know anyone who can do that on a sustained basis), value investing offers some opportunities to make money through the subdiscipline of investing in cyclical issues. Certain industries, ranging from steel to automobiles to financial services, tend to track ups and downs of business cycle. And expanding economy creates demand for cars, the demand for cars in turn demand for steel. As the auto makers and steel mills increase production, they make better use of their expensive factories, and their profit outlook improves. And of course, an improving profit outlook tend and with it an improving stock price. Similarly financial service companies- which use their money as their raw material- tend to enjoy higher profits as the cost of money (interest rates) go down and to be less profitable when interest rates go up. The trouble is predicting the course of the economy and interest rates is not simple. Get it wrong and you either buy cyclical stocks too late or hang on to them too long.

When the market is not in wholesale retreat, value investing becomes very difficult. By its nature, value investing often involves investing distressed companies. If they were not distressed, they would not be selling cheaply. The value investors hope is that a company can overcome whatever is causing the distress and rally back to health, taking its stock price with it. But there is a chance that it will not recover, that whatever is causing the problem brought the stock price low and will ultimately be fatal and the stock price will go to zero. That is one reason some of the most effective value investors tend to prefer large companies: Its simply harder to kill a huge company then a small one. Nevertheless, a dedicated value investor will shop among the smaller capitalization stocks in search for potential targets. It is more difficult to determine an intrinsic value for small or recently formed companies, but the lack of competition from every other potential buyer analyst on Wall Street at least affords an opportunity to find something interesting.

Different value investors use different ways to identify a possible stock to add to there portfolio. One of the most popular tools one that individuals can use fairly easily, is price to earnings ratio. The P/E ratio is merely the price per share of stock divided by annual earnings per share the company reported (trailing) or is expected to report (project). Generally, a P/E of 10 or less on trailing twelve months' earnings suggest that value investors should at least do some further analysis of the company. But they must do the work before they buy: there often is a fine reason that the P/E ratio is low, and it's to go lower.

When professional investors do find a company with a low P/E ratio that they feel is being unfairly penalized by the market they still do not necessarily buy the stock. Rather, they ask a basic question: If the stock undervalued, how long and what will it take for all other investors out there to realize it is a bid up the price so I can make a profit? If there is not a clear answer, the stock might not make it into the investor's portfolio. But if there is a catalyst, something looming that will bring the stock to the attention of other investors- a management shakeup, perhaps a new and improved version of the company's product- then it becomes a much more likely pick.

Yet for all their rational discipline, value investors have had a very tough time over the last decade or so. They argue that value stocks have not been" in style" amid the frenzy over the fast-growing technology and Internet stocks. Efficient market advocates, of course, argue that the market price is cyclical and that sick company stocks are exactly where they should be priced given what is known about them. Certainly, some of those companies and their stock will do very well. But others will not, and the trouble is nobody knows in advance which ones will and which ones will not, Meanwhile the market keeps marching higher, leaving the value investors studying Graham and Dodd, in its wake.

Growth Stocks: How High, How Fast?

Do not ask a growth stock investor to calculate intrinsic value of a company. She does not care. Ask her how fast earnings are growing, though, and she can tell you the percentage gains in each of the last eight or so quarters and give you projections on eight quarters yet to come. Earnings- specifically earnings growth- are the heart of growth stock investing. Earnings are growing fast. The stock will rise fast earning in a slump. The stock is going down. A stock with a price/earnings ratio of 60, a level that would give a value investor a heart attack, does not even phase your average growth investor if he or she can figure it going to 80. At its best growth stock investing will get you into the next Microsoft long before most people even heard of the company's name for the first time. At its worst, you can lose an awful lot of money awfully fast. At its best growth investing will take you on to the most exciting parts of the economy- technology, the Internet health care, or retailing example- where Big and sophisticated, and Innovative companies are talked about in awed tones and new companies with surprising products or new services are springing up constantly. At its worst, it will lead you into realm or the greater fool, a place ware you buy stock at a ridiculously high price on the presumption someone is even dumber and buy it from you for an even higher price.

Two concepts are central to every growth investor's analysis of a stock: The rate of earnings growth and the multiple the stock can command The rate of earnings can be understood two mean two things. First, it can be average pace at which earnings per share for a given company are growing. There is no set definition of what constitutes a growth stock, but many of the best and brightest money managers who follow the discipline focus on companies that are posting 20 percent per year increases per share earnings. Now 20 percent does not sound like such a huge number. But consider that at a rate of 20 percent a year a company's earnings will double in just for years. A small company growing at such furious pace will almost certainly encounter some sort of stumbling block: managing the expansion of factories, for example, or hiring and keeping quality employees (including managers). And a large company will face the monumental challenge of finding an ever-increasing supply of new customers and markets to conquer to maintain a 20 percent per year growth rate. Neither the small nor large company will find it goal to meet year after year. A disappoint over a quarter or an entire year will sadly disillusion investors, who almost certainly paid a premium price to obtain premium growth rate. Absent the premium growth rate, they will quickly bring the price down to something more appropriate.

The second definition of earnings growth involves acceleration. Investors looking for this kind of company want to see that rate of earnings growth rising in each quarter or year. They are looking for a company whose earnings that grew 5 percent in the second quarter over the first quarter, 10 percent in the third quarte over the second quarter, and 20 percent in the fourth quarter over the third quarter. In short, their looking for a company whose earnings profile, laid out a piece of graph paper, looks like the flight profile of a jet fighter going down a runway while climbing swiftly into the stratosphere. Needless to say, mathematics suggests that growth rates that are accelerating at that pace cannot be sustained for long. When they begin to slacken, as they evitable must the stock price follows a pattern closely akin to jet plane that runs out of fuel at fifty thousand feet. This subspeciality of growth stock investing is known as "momentum investing." It is not a game for the faint of heart, and because it requires extremely close attention to a company's business- virtually day-to-day monitoring- it is not something most individual should attempt.

Many growth investors use the price-earnings multiple a stock commands a tool roughly equivalent to the value investors intrinsic value, a way to measure a stock price against a benchmark. For example, a growth investor might compare the price earnings multiple of one semiconductor makes against the P/E of other semiconductors makers to help determine if the stock is desirable. If the P/E of the stock is the same as that of the average semiconductor maker's and the company's earnings growth rate is about in line with that of the rest of the industry, there would not be a compelling reason to buy the stock. But if the P/E were the same as the average semiconductors maker's and the company's earnings were growing faster, than a case could be made that the market will eventually assign a Higher P/E to the stock, allowing room for the stock price to rise.

Not surprisingly, semiconductor stocks probably will have an average P/E that is very Higher than the P/E of the average steel company, simply because the growth rat in those industries are quite different. The prize that many growth investors seek is a company in transition, shifting its business from that is valued at a low P/E multiple to one that is a High P/E multiple. A (very) Hypothetical example would be steel company that has found away to use its blast furnaces to make a semiconductor chip. A news of the discovery leaks out, growth investors will suddenly decide that the company's earnings will now suddenly grow at a rate similar to that of the other semiconductor makers rather than a rate of other steelmakers. Presto! The stock price can now rise tenfold and still be good buy, because earnings growth expectations have suddenly risen.

Such stories aren't common, but they do occur in more modest circumstances. One popular example occurred at the dawn of the personal computer. Suddenly the stock went from being valued as a retailer to being valued as a technology company. The lucky investor who had brought when it was thought to be a retailer got rich. Later Investors, who brought it when it was valued as a technology company, did not do as well, finding out the hard way that technology is a ruthlessly competitive business that changes almost day-to-day Tandy, now renamed Radio Shack, is back to being valued as a retailer

None of this suggest that investors cannot make money buying growth stocks. To the contrary, growth stocks investing can be immensely rewarding. Just ask anyone who bought Microsoft or Walmart ten years ago or Coca Cola twenty years ago. Those returns on those stocks have far exceeded those of the overall market. But I suspect that those same investors, aiming to diversity their portfolios, also bought lots of growth stocks at the same time but have not gone as fast or become as large as Microsoft, Wal-Mart -Coca Cola. And the money the have lost by betting on that growth has probably brought their average return over the last Ten or Twenty years pretty close two market average add in the costs of trading and the taxes they paid on gains, and they may even be below the markets average return.

Discussion with professional money managers and analysts who pursue a growth strategy suggest to me that the growth investing lend itself more easily than value investing to what, for lack of better term, I will call "story Investing." This approach simply calls for an investor to consider the story behind a company. The point as one manager puts it, is "to find a company that is so exciting, it will capture the imagination of other investors." Most recently the story du jour was the internet. Any company that made a plausible claim to have a business on or from the World Wide Web was instantly treated as having virtually unlimited growth potential. Amazon .com, Internet- based booksellers, was an early bene-ficiary of this particular story, and its stock rose so far and so fast that it was beyond the comprehension of many Wall Street professionals.

Some earlier story stocks have proven their worth over the years and even spawned variation on their based themes that have also proved profitable for investors. A case in point is Home Depot, the amazingly successful hardware and building and supply retailer that brought the "big box" concepts- a large store with a focus on a specific business that does sufficient volume to keep prices low- to the fore. To the fore. Home Depot created a nationwide network of large, well- staffed, and well stocked hardware and building supply stores. Staples did the same thing for the office supply business. But there have been abject failures of story stocks, too The Biotech industry, which is basically aims to sreate new drugs targeted at anything from curing cancer or AIDS to low-ering blood pressure, is littered with stories about promising drugs that when subjected to rigorous testing, failed to live up to their earlier promises, much to the regret and financial loss of many investors.

Of course, at any given moment you will not be only investor out there looking at the earnings growth rates and considering the stories behind atypical growth stock. Under just about any form of the efficient market hypothesis that I discussed early in this great chapter, the prices of the stocks that you are looking at will reflect to a great extent the combined judgements of all those other investors, leaving you in the same fix you were in when you considered value stocks: finding the few stocks that will be real winners while avoiding those that will be losers.

Narrowing the Field: Market Capitalization
Value and growth investing are two broadest methods by which professional investors describe their approach to stock picking. To future narrow the range of stocks from which they choose their portfolio components, many pros clas-

sify their styles by the size of the stock they research. Size, in this case, refers to the market capitalization of a company, which is merely the per-share price multiplied by the number of shares outstanding. If for example a company has 100 million shares outstanding (that, is it has at some time in the past sold 100million shares to the investing public) and those shares are trading at $5 a share, the company is said to have a "market cap" of $500 million. Some money managers prefer to invest in small stocks and others prefer large cap issues. While there is no official arbiter of what constitutes "small" and large" stocks, The Wall Street Journal currently sets the dividing point at a market cap of $1.5 billion, Any company with a market cap of less than that is to be considered small stock, and any to have a larger market cap is to be considered a large company. Some money recognizers that there is an awfully wide gulf between a 'large' company with a market cap of $1.6 billion and a company like Microsoft, with a market cap of $390 billion differentiate themselves as "midcap" investors who generally confine themselves to stocks with a market cap of between $1.5 billion and $5 billion.

From professional money managers" point of view there are advantages and disadvantages to each size category. Large cap stocks tend to be well established companies, although they can certainly be experiencing problems at any given time. More to the point, though they will relatively large "float," or numbers of shares outstanding, and thus usually more "liquid," or easily traded, than much smaller stock. For example, if you wanted to buy or sell one hundred thousand shares of General Motors at any given moment, there is a good chance the transaction could be done in a matter of minutes because GM is a highly liquid stock.

Large stocks have another advantage over small stocks. Bluntly put, it is power One need look no further than the government's recent antitrust case against Microsoft to witness that power. The company brought enormous influence to bring on suppliers, customers, and even governments to get what it wanted. Even a big company gets into trouble, the economics and political clout it wields will often get it benefits that can stave of or ameliorate the worst effects of whatever the problem its having. As I pointed out earlier value investors often prefer large companies because they are simply much more difficult to kill.

But large stocks seem to get far more attention from Wall Street. Batteries of analysts are constantly poking and probing a company like General Electric, trying to determine how each of its many businesses is doing and to predict accurately what the company will earn each quarter, for anyone who believes in the efficient market hypothesis, that is not good news. It leaves little room for the average investor to discover any inefficiencies that can be used to make an outsize profit.

Finally, large companies generally have a difficult time growing at above average rates. Even the best- run big companies cannot achieve average annual growth rates of more than about 20 percent for any sustained period of time, and the vast majority are far below that.

Small stocks tends to be very different. The typical small company is relatively young and not well established, but more important, it usually has a relatively small float. A professional money manager who decides to buy hundred thousand shares of a small company will find not only that it takes hours or maybe days to accomplish the transaction, but also that in the course of buying or selling it becomes obvious to others in the market that something unusual is happening to the stock, causing them to try to take advantage of it. The results may be that when a money manager begins adding a small stock to a portfolio the price quickly rises from say, $12 a share to $14 a share.

Small companies often have little power. Customers pressure them for price concessions and play them of against one another. Suppliers worry whether small companies will pay their bills on time, and small companies rarely have much, If any clout with the government. Hundreds of small public companies fail every year, resulting in total losses for investors who owned the stock.

But there are advantages to being small, at least from a potential stockholder's point of view. Small companies can grow incredibly fast, at least in the first few years of their evolution toward becoming a big company. Since analysts follow small companies, it appears that there probably is a better chance for an individual investor to discover unrealized value here than in the large-cap universe. Cite: Winning with The Market, Beat the Traders and The Brokers in Good Times and Bad, Douglas R. Sease pg.58 – pgs.73

Author

My name is DAVID CHRISTOPHER PLATT born on Canada day and received a Medallion on July 1,1967. Popular for there fine foods and pastries, and Aubon coffee. The language fluently spoke in Montreal the province of Quebec is French and shops and business are there for window shopping or if you just want to go out and get some clean fresh air and just to take in some of that Canadian hospitality, that makes it worth the while to get out get some clean fresh air and get some shopping done.

Artwork different trend that mainstreams this ever so popular and Historical city Mosaic trends to look for and a colossal of designers a lot of new world design, and of work and cultural designs, and French cuisine they have to offer.

Me and the rest of my family are out of New York, ny, My Mom Frances Platt is from Spring Valley New York, and my Father Calvin Is from New York from Monsey, New York, then moved from there to upstate New York to the town of Washingtonville, New York and lived in a nice family house country type of living outside the 'BIG' city.

Then headed down to sunny south Florida where we lived in a suburb outside the city over 30 years now, the weather is nice and if you are looking towards pursuing on furthering your education or going back to school Florida is a very good place to be to further your education or go back to school for a higher education a Degree, or Internship.

Reference

Getting the job you really want, sixth edition a step by step guide to finding a good job in less time c 2011 by JIST Publishing

RESUMES, ELECTRONIC FILING

JIST PUBLISHERS, JISTCARDS and services

Edx – David Christopher Platt Micro Master of Business Program M.B.A.

Fifth Edition Business Analysis with Microsoft Excel - Conrad Carlsberg